BOOK FOR TEENS

by Gracie Carroll

**Copyright 2021 @ Gracie Carroll
All Rights Reserved.**

No part of this publications may be reproduced, distributed, or transmitted in any form or by any means, including photocopying, recording, other electronic, or mechanical methods.

For any inquiries or questions regarding our books, please contact us at : **graciecarrol@yahoo.com**

ISBN: 9798585837142

HOW TO PLAY.

The rules of this game is very simple.

To Start The Game:

- You need at least TWO players.

- Choose the first one.
  He/She will choose the question for the next player.

- All questions begin with the phrase "Would You Rather...?" and ends with two possible funny or thought-provoking scenarios to choose from.

- Next should pick an answer from two given scenarios.

> ## The Main thing is to pick something
>
> ## One can't answer "both" or "none".

- You can play until you have creative ideas or untill someone won't be able to make a choice.

The only rule that cannot be broken is that of having fun!

REMEMBER!

The questions and scenarios presented in this book solely for entertainment purposes only.

And should NOT be taken seriously!

HAVE A NICE GAME!

LET'S START.

WOULD YOU RATHER....

fall asleep during class

fall asleep during lunch?

have a fun teacher who is bad at teaching

have a mean teacher who is really effective at teaching?

WOULD YOU RATHER....

Have an annoying but smart lab partner

-OR-

Have a fun but lazy lab partner?

Be the best athlete in school

-OR-

Be the smartest student in school?

WOULD YOU RATHER....

Walk to school

Take the bus to school?

Miss your prom

Miss your graduation?

WOULD YOU RATHER....

Have your teachers like you more

-OR-

Have your classmates like you more?

Have a bad yearbook picture

-OR-

Have a lame yearbook quote?

WOULD YOU RATHER....

Be Prom King/Queen

-OR-

Be the valedictorian?

Teach a class at your school

-OR-

Have one of your parents be your teacher?

WOULD YOU RATHER....

Go to a day school

Go to a boarding school?

Go to college

Go back to kindergarten?

WOULD YOU RATHER....

Go to your dream college and have lots of debt

-OR-

Go to mediocre college and have no debt?

Get a full time job

-OR-

Go to college?

WOULD YOU RATHER....

Get home schooled

Go to public school?

Cheat on a test and pass

Fail a test with your integrity intact?

WOULD YOU RATHER....

Lose 5 friends

Gain 2 enemies?

Have weird friends

Have weird siblings?

WOULD YOU RATHER....

Find true love

Win 5 million dollars?

Be single for the rest of your life

Have your parents pick your future spouse?

WOULD YOU RATHER....

Have lots of siblings

-OR-

Be the only child?

Get dumped through a text

-OR-

Get dumped in front of your friends?

WOULD YOU RATHER....

Date someone with a great personality

-OR-

Date the best looking person in school?

Know lots of people but not be close to them

-OR-

Have 1 really good friend?

WOULD YOU RATHER....

Spend a day without your phone but around other people

-OR-

Spend a day completely alone but with your phone

Be the oldest child

-OR-

Be the youngest child?

WOULD YOU RATHER....

Get married at 20

Get married at 50?

Have a really big family

Have a super small family?

WOULD YOU RATHER....

Have friends that are smarter than you

Have friends that are better looking than you?

Have lots of money

Have lots of good friends?

WOULD YOU RATHER....

Forget to wear socks

-OR-

Forget to wear underwear?

Wear clothes that are too small

-OR-

Wear clothes that are too big?

WOULD YOU RATHER....

Wear winter clothes all year

Wear summer clothes all year?

Have everyone wear school uniforms

Have everyone wear whatever they want to school?

WOULD YOU RATHER....

Dress for looks

Dress for comfort?

Wear dirty underwear

Wear underwear with holes in it?

WOULD YOU RATHER....

Wear your clothes inside out

-OR-

Wear your clothes backward?

Become an adult overnight

-OR-

Stay a teenager forever?

WOULD YOU RATHER....

Give up your phone

Give up junk food?

Be a bully

Be bullied?

WOULD YOU RATHER....

Have fun now but work really hard later

Work hard now but enjoy life later?

Lose all of your hair

Lose all of your teeth?

WOULD YOU RATHER....

Have nosey parents

-OR-

Have strict parents?

Get a big pimple on your nose

-OR-

Trip in front of the entire school?

WOULD YOU RATHER....

Give a speech in front of the whole school

Clean all the bathrooms at school everyday for a week

Gossip about your best friend

Have your best friend gossip about you?

WOULD YOU RATHER....

Have 10 kids in the future

-OR-

Have no kids at all?

Snore when you sleep

-OR-

Talk in your sleep?

WOULD YOU RATHER....

Be awkward

Have all your friends be awkward?

Have all your teeth fall out

Have all your hair fall out?

WOULD YOU RATHER....

Get grounded for a month

-OR-

Get kicked out of your home for a month?

Shave your head

-OR-

Let your hair grow down to your ankles?

WOULD YOU RATHER....

Accidentally swallow gum

-OR-

Accidentally get gum stuck in your hair?

Get a really bad birthday gift

-OR-

Receive no birthday gift at all?

WOULD YOU RATHER....

Drink juice

Drink soda?

Eat cafeteria food

Bring food from home?

WOULD YOU RATHER....

Wake up early and eat breakfast

Sleep in and skip breakfast?

Eat only veggies for a week

Eat only fruit for a week?

WOULD YOU RATHER....

Learn how to bake

-OR-

Learn how to cook?

Start a food fight

-OR-

Start a pillow fight?

WOULD YOU RATHER....

Do the laundry for your family

-OR-

Cook dinner for your family?

Never watch TV again

-OR-

Never play video games?

WOULD YOU RATHER....

Listen to music with headphones

-OR-

Listen to music on a speaker?

Listen to the same song for a year

-OR-

Only be allowed to watch the same movie for a year?

WOULD YOU RATHER....

Be a famous movie star

-OR-

Be a famous musician?

Play sports

-OR-

Watch sports?

WOULD YOU RATHER....

Be a cat

Be a dog?

End crime

End poverty?

WOULD YOU RATHER....

Sneeze really hard but quietly

-OR-

Sneeze gently but very loudly?

Look like a dog

-OR-

Smell like a dog?

WOULD YOU RATHER....

Travel back 1 year in time

Travel forward 1 year in time?

Be a fast writer

Be a fast reader?

WOULD YOU RATHER....

Moo like a cow after every time you say something

Quack like a duck after every time you say something?

Have a pillow fight

Have a snowball fight?

WOULD YOU RATHER....

Save the world from an alien invasion

Save the world from a terrible disease?

Sit between 2 really big people

Sit between 2 really smelly people?

WOULD YOU RATHER....

Have a big bed
in a small bedroom

Have a small bed
in a big bedroom?

Sneak out of the house

Miss out on the party
of the year?

WOULD YOU RATHER....

Use someone else's toothbrush

Find out someone else used your toothbrush?

Live in Narnia

go to school at Hogwarts?

WOULD YOU RATHER....

have only two close friends

-OR-

many acquaintances?

be known as the best student in your school

-OR-

be the captain of one of the sports teams?

WOULD YOU RATHER....

date someone unattractive with a great personality

-OR-

date someone very attractive with a bad personality?

live an extra 25 years

-OR-

live a life without the need to sleep?

WOULD YOU RATHER....

be able to teleport anywhere

-OR-

be able to read minds?

have the ability to rewind to a previous time in your life

-OR-

have the ability to fast forward to a later time in your life?

WOULD YOU RATHER....

have to end every sentence with a racial slur

have to drop two f-bombs in every sentence?

go on a double date with your parents

with your partner's parents?

WOULD YOU RATHER....

have slow but unlimited Internet

-OR-

paid but limited Internet?

burp confetti

-OR-

fart glitter?

WOULD YOU RATHER....

give up AC and heating for the rest of your life

give up the Internet for the rest of your life?

be able to read minds

to predict the future?

WOULD YOU RATHER....

look 10 years older from the neck up

the neck down?

have 20 million YouTube subscribers

produce a blockbuster action movie?

WOULD YOU RATHER....

lose the ability to read

-OR-

lose the ability to speak?

kill one human being

-OR-

50 baby animals?

WOULD YOU RATHER....

be born in the past

in the future?

only use TikTok
for the rest of your life

only use YouTube
or the rest of your life?

WOULD YOU RATHER....

get completely drunk after one alcoholic drink

never be able to get drunk?

be in jail for five years

be in a coma for five years?

WOULD YOU RATHER....

know how you die

when you die?

flirt with your crush using emojis while texting

using memes while texting?

WOULD YOU RATHER....

have all dogs try to attack you when they see you

all birds try to attack you when they see you?

share your home with a bunch of rats

live with your parents forever?

WOULD YOU RATHER....

dip your foot in acid

set your foot on fire?

have all of your shirts one size too small

have all of your shirts two sizes too big?

WOULD YOU RATHER....

clog the toilet at your workplace (school)

-OR-

at your crush's house?

be able to remember everything you see

-OR-

remember everything you hear?

WOULD YOU RATHER....

always look like you are 8 months pregnant

always have a black eye?

stop showering

stop brushing your teeth?

WOULD YOU RATHER....

only be able to speak via a translator

only speak when asked a question?

not wear shoes for the rest of your life

not drive a car for the rest of your life?

WOULD YOU RATHER....

be captured by a wild tribe in the jungle

be captured by pirates at sea?

pee in a litter box

drink a cup of toilet water?

WOULD YOU RATHER....

be naked all the time

-OR-

never leave your house/apartment?

have a beer belly

-OR-

have three chins?

WOULD YOU RATHER....

be unable to wash
your hair for a month

shave your legs
for a month?

always fart in colors

always fart loudly?

WOULD YOU RATHER....

have a head the size of a tennis ball

-OR-

have a head the size of a watermelon?

only wear used underwear

-OR-

only use strangers' toothbrushes?

WOULD YOU RATHER....

have the brightness on your phone stuck on low

-OR-

the volume on your phone stuck on low?

pee every time you stand up

-OR-

poop every time you sit down?

WOULD YOU RATHER....

wear the same socks for a month

the same underwear for a week?

get diarrhea on a first date

run into your parents on a first date?

WOULD YOU RATHER....

have hands that kept growing as you got older

have feet that kept growing as you got older?

always feel like you have to sneeze

always feel like you have to poop?

WOULD YOU RATHER....

find $5 on the ground

find all of your missing socks?

every shirt you wear to be itchy

only be able to use one ply of toilet paper?

WOULD YOU RATHER....

have an elephant-sized hamster

a hamster-sized elephant?

take cold showers every day for the rest of your life

eat only cold food for the rest of your life?

WOULD YOU RATHER....

never wash your sheets ever again

-OR-

only be able to shower once every two weeks?

have eyes the size of a baseball

-OR-

have eyes the size of a pea?

WOULD YOU RATHER....

eat a dead rat

eat 20 live spiders?

be allergic to babies

be allergic to elderly people?

WOULD YOU RATHER....

lose all your memories

go blind?

have supernatural strength

have supernatural intelligence?

WOULD YOU RATHER....

never be able to go out during the day

during the night?

control your dreams

watch them the next day?

WOULD YOU RATHER....

have a horrible short-term memory

-OR-

have a horrible long-term memory?

live with no electronics

-OR-

live with no friends?

WOULD YOU RATHER....

always speak all your thoughts out loud

never speak again (even in sign language)?

be alone for the rest of your life

always be surrounded by annoying people?

WOULD YOU RATHER....

infinite battery life for your phone

-OR-

infinite fuel for your car?

have a completely automated home

-OR-

have a self-driving car?

WOULD YOU RATHER....

never be able to watch Netflix

Youtube again?

get away with lying every time

always know when someone is lying?

Printed in the USA
CPSIA information can be obtained
at www.ICGtesting.com
LVHW021142161124
796822LV00009B/158